The Practical Guide to Multicultural Marketing

Best Practices for Planning and Implementing In-Language Market Strategies

By
Natalie Rouse
and
Adriana Waterston

Blue Dragon Publishing

Published by Blue Dragon Publishing

Williamsburg, VA

www.blue-dragon-publishing.com

Copyright © 2012, 2017

by Natalie Rouse and Adriana Waterston

ISBN 978-0-9832454-6-9

ISBN 978-1-939696-03-8 (ePub)

Cover by LahDeeDah Marketing

Table of Contents

Chapter 1:
Why Are You Reading This Handbook?

Congratulations! If you are reading this handbook, it's likely you have recently been charged by your company to work on its multicultural marketing initiatives – and for good reason! Over the past few years, multicultural marketing has evolved from a low budget tactic designed to meet a particular business challenge to a cornerstone of many major corporations' overall strategic plans for future success.

The 2000 Census had a large impact on the growth of multicultural marketing as a major business focus. Before the U.S. Census Bureau released the 2000 data documenting the incredible growth of America's non-white populations, America's multicultural, multilingual consumers were virtually invisible within the framework of the "general (read: white, non-Hispanic) market."

With the exception of companies that operate in specific, niche, Black, Hispanic or Asian markets, multicultural consumers were rarely on the radar of major corporations at all. Similarly, for many, stereotypes and assumptions such as "multicultural consumers have no money to spend, so we should not market to them" and "multicultural consumers are not in the market for my (cars, or banking services, or cable television services, or consumer goods...)" justified inaction when it came to reaching out to America's multicultural populations.

Census 2010 data further asserted what the 2000 Census showed us about the growing numbers and economic and political clout of America's ethnic and racial "minorities." We now have even more eye-opening proof of the changing face of America's demographics; as of Census 2010, over one-third (36%) of the country's population is Hispanic, Black, Asian, or some other non-white group. Today, 16% of our country's population is of Hispanic origin; 13% is Black; 5% is Asian or Pacific Islander; and 6% report some other, non-white race.

Notably, the Census reports there were about 40 million foreign-born persons living in the United States as of 2010 (a number which is likely an undercount). Over half (53%) of the foreign-born population is from Latin America, while about 1 in 3 (28%) are from just Asia. More detailed information about the foreign-born population can be gleaned on the Census website. This link will lead you to the 2010 Census brief titled, "The Foreign Born Population in the United States:" *http://www.census.gov/prod/2012pubs/acs-19.pdf*.

Multicultural marketing has come a long way since Census 2000, but in many ways the field is still in its infancy. First, marketing, advertising and research budgets for multicultural marketing are still minuscule compared to the budgets allotted to "general market" consumers. Second, companies new to the multicultural market have little in the way of guidance as far as best practices and roadmaps for success; and that's where this handbook comes in!

One thing is for sure: Succeeding in multicultural marketing is not a simple process.

First, who is your real target? Successful multicultural marketing takes into account that ethnic communities in America are not homogeneous, nor are they stagnant. Within each larger segment there exists a great deal of diversity, and this diversity is dynamic and constantly changing. Some examples include the following:

➢ Language usage (i.e. what language they speak at home, in which language they consume the most media, and an individual's personal fluency with English compared to the native tongue);

➤ Country of origin (we have come across people who assumed all Asians are Chinese, or all Hispanics are Mexican!);

➤ Nativity and generations (i.e. whether someone is foreign-born or born in the U.S., how long they have lived in the U.S., and how many generations of their family have been here);

➤ The degree of their affinities to their heritage and culture versus an "American" culture; and of course,

➤ The standard demographic and psychographic characteristics marketers have always used to segment the "general market."

Secondly, what resources do you have? In order to succeed at multicultural marketing, a company needs to make a real commitment of both budget and time and must have a team with the ability to think creatively and "outside the box" in order to tap the true potential of these important consumer segments.

Thirdly and most importantly, success requires cultural and linguistic sensitivity and knowledge.

That is where we come in. The goal of this handbook is to provide marketers like you with the best tips and strategies for multicultural marketing, specifically, in-language ethnic marketing. We will guide you through the step-by-step process of launching an ethnically targeted and in-language campaign, which is an important element of multicultural marketing. This handbook will provide ideas to guide you in completing the process.

> Identifying and quantifying the market opportunity and making the business case internally.
> Reaching out and establishing a presence within the community.

- Putting your plan into action by designing and rolling out a successful marketing campaign.
- Implementing and Executing, including product, brand positioning, and creative execution.
- Following through by putting your customer care tools and systems in place to meet demand.
- Reporting and monitoring by applying best practices for measuring and tracking the success of your campaign.

With all of this information, it is important to keep in mind that an in-language strategy cannot be the only component of your multicultural marketing efforts. To be truly successful, you will need to develop a comprehensive strategy that takes into account all segments of your target audience. For example, not every Hispanic speaks Spanish or watches Spanish language TV. A solely Spanish language campaign will exclude a very large and powerful segment of the Hispanic market—U.S. born Hispanics. These U.S born Hispanics include young people who are very involved in mainstream, English language media. The same holds true for each and every multicultural group in America. Moving forward, holistic strategies that recognize multiculturalism as a hallmark of 21st century America will be the standard. Within such holistic strategies, in-language tactics will continue to play an important role.

Chapter 2:
Identify and Quantify the Market Opportunity: Making the Business Case Internally

Ready, Set...Go?

Your company has taken the first major step; they've hired you! Now what?

Your first step is NOT TO TAKE ANYTHING FOR GRANTED. The fact that your company has hired you— and perhaps given you some specific business goals— does not necessarily mean it will be an easy path internally. Many multicultural marketers quickly learn that while the intention may be there, companies are often not quite ready to put their money or their resources where their mouths are when it comes to multicultural marketing. What kind of budget will you have? What kind of interdepartmental support is there? Is there a staff, or will you be working independently? Finally, are the goals you have been given realistic for your market? Managing expectations is always a good exercise.

The good news is that often the return on the investment in multicultural communities is greater than you might have in the general market. There are many reasons for this:

➢ This is probably the first time your company has made a serious effort to reach out to these consumers. If you do it right, they will reward you for paying attention;

➢ Ethnic media is generally less expensive than the general market, so you get more "bang for your buck";

➢ Grassroots events and outreach are great ways to reach ethnic communities, and these tactics can be extremely low-cost;

➢ Done correctly, using cultural and linguistic touchstones for marketing can resonate in extremely meaningful and memorable ways;

➢ In tight ethnic communities, especially those with a large number of immigrant and in-language populations, word of mouth plays an important role;

➢ Anecdotal evidence suggests some ethnic communities tend to be more brand-loyal than the general market; and

➢ If you are lucky, your competitors have not entered this market yet!

Making the Business Case

A good first step is to put together a presentation that makes the business case internally for multicultural marketing. The goal is to answer concisely the basic questions: Who? Why? What? How? When? Where? Here is a guideline on the kinds of facts, figures and information helpful in executing a strong and effective business case presentation. Much of this information can be obtained by visiting the websites of the U.S. Census Bureau, the Pew Research Center, your local government, and local organizations.

Who?

➢ Get a snapshot of your local market or markets: Using Census and other data sources to provide an overview of the demographics in your market. Remember, a lot has happened in a very short period of time. What might have been the demographic characteristics of a certain place even just four years ago most certainly changed, perhaps even drastically.

➢ Analyze the data by community pockets: Where, specifically, do each of these demographic groups live?

➢ Gather data on language use: How many are foreign-born and speak primarily their native language? How many are bilingual and bicultural? How many are fully acculturated and English speaking? How many are second or third generation and beyond?

Why?

- Get a snapshot of the business opportunity, including buying power and other socioeconomic data.
- Determine the projected growth of these communities compared to the general market in your local geographic area.
- Assess how this ethnic community compares in terms of other demographics that make them compelling: median age, number of children in the home, average disposable income, etc.
- Analyze how your company or product is currently indexing among these ethnic communities.
- Research what your competitors are doing, how they are implementing their strategies and what is working for them (or not).

What?

➢ Identify your goals for each ethnic community in your local market or markets.

➢ Pinpoint who within this community is your target: the in-language population, the bicultural and bilingual population, or the acculturated population. Why or why not? State what specific goals you have for each of those subgroups.

How?

➢ Detail the ethnic media outlets available.

➢ Research the grassroots cultural events, organizations and other methods of outreach you can use.

➢ Create a summary of the overall strategy, including examples of possible tactics to implement.

When?

➢ Set your timeline for action, measurement and success.

Chapter 3:
Reach Out: Establishing a Presence within the Community

The most successful multicultural marketing strategies do not simply come from marketers sitting in cubicles or corporate offices all day. In order to establish credibility with your potential customers and become intimately familiar with what makes your target market click, you need to reach out to, learn about, interact with, and establish a presence within the community you are hoping to serve. This is a crucial step for both your company, and for you, as a budding multicultural marketer.

You probably already know that many communities don't necessarily consume general market media and often don't respond to general marketing tactics in the same fashion as their "general market" counterparts. So how will you most effectively be able to reach out? We will explore this further in Chapter 3, but until then it's essential to know that one of the most important ways is to get involved on a "grassroots" level. When making your business case, you outline the ethnic media, grassroots events and organizations that exist in your target community. Well, now it's time to get out there and meet them face-to-face! Start subscribing to, listening to, and watching the media (print, radio, web, TV) that exerts the greatest influence in this community. Get involved with community-based organizations (CBOs) and become friendly with the cultural and business leaders who are most respected and powerful. Start frequenting the religious, social, and food establishments that are most popular. Make sure you don't miss the cultural rituals, festivals, and events that take place during the year.

As you begin the process, don't forget that none of us live in a silo. We all live and thrive in the general market world as well. It is likely there are also non-ethnic media, establishments, and events that are popular among these ethnic consumers. Be careful not to make the mistake of stereotyping or being essentialist in your thinking, as this could cause you to miss some important opportunities to reach out.

By interacting with the community and experiencing the culture first-hand, you will become a better marketer. You will be able to recognize and create more culturally sound materials and tactics. You will understand your competitive environment—how the other players are approaching the market and how they are perceived. You will develop a contextual understanding of what motivates and influences consumer choices. Finally, you will have a better understanding of how to improve the customer experience when you finally engage them to buy your product or service.

The following are examples of great ways to learn about your target audience:

> Community Centers: Many ethnic groups have their own community centers. These centers have membership lists you can buy (or even get free) for mailings, bulletin boards on which you can place your flyers or brochures, events at which you can have a presence with a table or booth, and other opportunities for reaching the community they serve.

> Chambers of Commerce: The Hispanic Chamber of Commerce and the U.S. Pan-Asian Chamber of Commerce are national organizations that have chapters all over the country. There are also independent Pan-Asian Chambers of Commerce as well as chambers of commerce for specific ethnic groups (for example, the Puerto Rican Chambers of Commerce, French-

American Chambers of Commerce, German-American Chambers of Commerce, Chinese Chambers of Commerce or Japanese Chambers of Commerce). A quick Internet search will reveal whether there is a relevant chamber of commerce in your market. Their events and websites are excellent venues, not only to promote your product or service but also to connect with community leaders who can really help you build bridges and relationships within the community.

➢ Embassies and Consulates: Embassies (usually located in Washington, DC or New York) and Consulates (in other key markets) often host events and "meet and greets." Both are excellent places to establish important political connections within the community you wish to serve. The Embassy and Consulate websites often offer a wealth of information about the country's culture, politics, and population (in the US and in local markets), as well as information about upcoming cultural events.

➢ Local churches/religious institutions: People in ethnic communities often have strong ties to their local churches or other religious institutions. In addition to religious services, these institutions often host events and fundraisers; and some even have charity arms that can always use sponsors and support. Many have newsletters and community bulletin boards where you can place ads. Reaching out to these local religious institutions is an excellent way to instill goodwill within the target community, while also increasing your company's exposure.

➢ Local businesses: Where do people in the community shop? Where do they eat? Where do they do laundry? Which movie theatre do they visit? Which are the popular hair salons in the area? These are all excellent places to reach your potential customers through the distribution of flyers or promotional materials or to partner with other local businesses.

➢ <u>Local ethnic or community websites</u>: Don't make the mistake of assuming ethnic consumers are not high-tech and do not use the web. In fact, the web is an important tool many ethnic consumers use to keep culturally connected with what is going on in their home countries and to keep in touch with friends and family in other countries (for example, via services like Skype). They also use the web for establishing new connections, accessing resources, and getting information about their local area. Find creative ways to establish a presence on these sites—not just through advertising, but also through blogging, forums, posting press releases, and other types of public relations (PR)/outreach initiatives.

Getting Involved with Community-Based Organizations (CBO's)

In each community, there are often many community-based organizations—large and small— that are extremely influential. The most obvious example of these are the Chambers of Commerce, mentioned earlier, that often host mixers and events for business leaders in the community.

Finding out about the organizations in your community may seem like a challenge, but think about it as a large social network. If you identify one CBO, it will be able to refer you to others. Once you get a lay of the land as far as which organizations are out there, start attending their functions and events. Then you'll be able to meet and network with those members of the community who are most influential and knowledgeable, relationships that will prove to be invaluable as you strive to learn more about the community and culture.

Another key reason to become involved with CBO's and community leaders is the opportunity to find potential business partners with whom you can work for your mutual success. If you work for a major consumer or media brand, your company may have certain caché or clout and a budget that a local business or CBO may not. They, on the other hand, know their community better than you do, are respected within the community, and have a direct line of communication to the community —valuable assets your corporate dollars just can't buy. Think about it: "word of mouth" and having a respected leader or organization behind you can make or break your success in this space.

It might sound a bit daunting to put yourself out there at these events, especially if you don't know anyone in the community yet or if you tend to be shy. Here's author Natalie's advice, based on her experiences getting involved with the local Chinese Chambers of Commerce:

Natalie's notes:

I've found one of the best ways to inform and educate the local Chinese community about the products I'm marketing is to meet them face-to-face. I make the effort to join the local Chinese Chamber of Commerce, for example, and attend some of their mixers. This gives me a chance to meet other business leaders from the community, who often prove to be very valuable contacts.

When I first started working in Asian marketing, I found attending these kinds of events gave me another advantage: I was able to gather insight into the culture I was trying to target. At first it was hard, but I soon realized I didn't have to feel awkward just because I was the only non-Chinese person at the event. I found others admired my efforts and were extremely warm, inviting, and helpful to me.

As a newcomer in the community, it won't be expected that you know all of the customs of that community; but you should do some research before showing up at an event, especially to make sure you do not show any disrespect. For example, when meeting a Chinese or Japanese businessperson and exchanging business cards, it is customary to receive their card by accepting it with both hands and a slight bow. This action signals mutual respect. The same gesture is used when you present your business card to them: two hands and a slight bow.

During the event, one of the biggest mistakes you can make is to be too anxious to network and tell everyone about your company and the products and services you provide. This can be perceived as pushy. We recommend not rushing into a sales pitch until they open the door by asking you about your business. Presumably, your first event in this community won't be your last—there will be plenty of opportunities to sell yourself and your company later. Remember, "People want to know how much you care before they care how much you know."

Getting Involved with Community Events

Take stock of the local, religious, and cultural events that take place throughout the year and are attended by members of your target community. Purchase a booth, become a sponsor, and work hard to make sure you have a meaningful physical presence there. These local events usually do not cost much compared to traditional advertising but are just as crucial to your marketing plan. The direct and immediate benefit of participating in these events is that you gain visibility and build brand recognition. That being said, there are other less tangible, yet even more important, reasons to be there. Your presence speaks volumes to the members of the community about how important they are to you. It's more than a symbolic gesture—it's you extending your hand in the first effort to build a relationship. Over time, your regular presence and support will generate trust, loyalty, and goodwill in a way that print, TV ads, and direct mail pieces can never do.

Listed below are a few holidays and festivals that are celebrated by different ethnic groups. This is just the tip of the iceberg. Getting to know the community you wish to serve will include becoming intimately familiar with all of the community's most relevant holidays and finding ways to incorporate them into your outreach plan.

➢ Lunar New Year – Chinese, Vietnamese, Korean
➢ India Independence - Indian
➢ Filipino Independence – Philippino

- Cinco de Mayo and Mexican Independence Day- Mexican
- Pre-Independence Day and Independence Day- Argentinian
- Carnaval – Brasilina, Latino
- Autumn Moon – Chinese
- Eid – Muslim
- Iftar banquets during the Islamic month of Ramadan - Muslim
- Puerto Rican Day Parade (many heavily Puerto Rican markets have their own Puerto Rican day parades but the largest is in New York City, and is televised in other major Puerto Rican markets).

Sounds easy, right? Well, it can be, just make sure you follow these basic rules of thumb:

Don't just sponsor. Have an on-site presence!

Your logo on a banner or on the back of a T-shirt only takes you so far. Being present onsite is an opportunity to educate potential customers about your products and services. It allows them to taste, smell, see, and feel what your product is all about and provides an opportunity to build "buzz" and "hype" around your company. Plus, it allows you an "inside look" at the community you are hoping to serve.

Don't just have a booth. Make sure your booth actually has living, breathing people at it!

One of the biggest mistakes a company can make is to have a booth or table with collateral and brochures, yet no company representation in sight. The message you are sending with this is, "We'll throw some money at this, but we don't want to waste our TIME." Your support of the event just backfired—and you may not get a second chance to make a first impression.

Don't just have living, breathing people at your booth. Make sure they can connect culturally and linguistically with the attendees!

It makes sense to staff your booth with people who are connected culturally to the event you are sponsoring. For example, if you are sponsoring a Hispanic event, try to recruit some of your Hispanic employees to staff the booth. Most importantly, when participating at events that will be largely attended by non-English speakers, make sure someone at your booth can speak the language.

If you do not have someone on your staff that speaks the language, don't worry! Get in touch with the event organizers, and they may be able to connect you with a volunteer who can work at your booth with your staff.

<u>Don't just have someone who can speak the language.</u> Have someone who can sell your brand!

Don't make the mistake of staffing your booth with temp workers who fit the bill because they are from the community or speak the language if they can't adequately represent your company. Make sure you send strong, outgoing staff from your company who will represent you and can work alongside any in-language volunteers to ensure your booth visitors leave with the right information about your products and services.

<u>Don't just wait until they come to your booth to sell your brand.</u> Generate some buzz!

Once you've made the investment in time and resources to participate at a local or community event, put your marketing hat on and think outside the box to come up with creative ways to draw attention to your booth. Remember, cultural sensitivity is important; what might be appropriate at a Las Vegas trade show may not fly at ethnic cultural events that are often family-oriented.

Natalie's notes:

> *If you're at a festival-type of event where there are many booths and a lot of traffic on the grounds, you want to have something that catches the attendees' attention—so it really has to be relevant. For example, at a South Asian event, a raffle for baseball tickets would not be*

appealing, but tickets to a cricket match would be a huge hit. On the other hand, at a Japanese event if you were offering baseball tickets, you'd probably have a line of people in front of your booth!

<u>Don't just create a buzz</u>. Leverage partnerships to make the most out of your presence at events!

Think about other, non-multicultural marketing relationships your company has that you can tap into to generate even more excitement around your participation in the cultural or community event. For example, if your company sponsors a sports team, consider whether any of the players on the team would be a good fit as a celebrity guest at your booth to sign autographs (i.e., a Japanese baseball player at a Japanese event, a Dominican baseball player at a Hispanic event, etc.). Or, if you have an existing marketing relationship with an airline, why not raffle off a pair of tickets to Paris when you're at a French cultural event? You get the idea.

Chapter 4:
Put Your Plan into Action: Designing a Successful Marketing Campaign

You've done your homework. Now it's time to get the job done!

To execute a multicultural marketing campaign, you'll need to follow some basic steps. These may not seem that different from the steps you might follow for the general market, but the devil is in the details!

Step 1:
Identifying the Objectives

Having a clear picture of your objectives and a specific measure of success is a key part of this process. Intangible goals like "establishing goodwill in the community," are much harder to quantify than tangible ones like "selling 5,000 widgets via an in-language campaign."

Is the campaign you are implementing strategic or tactical? Is there a specific business/sales goal you want to achieve, or is the objective of this campaign more broad in scope, such as a rebranding? What do you want to sell and to whom are you communicating? If there is a specific sales objective, what are your projected sales goals?

And finally, you must take your budget into consideration when setting your objectives. You must be realistic in what you can accomplish with the money allotted.

Step 2: Finding Marketing and Advertising Partners

Choosing an Agency

It might be tempting to turn to your general market agency to help you execute your multicultural marketing materials, but do your homework first to make sure it really has multicultural capabilities and particular expertise with the community you want to reach.

Finding experts who really know your target audience is key to implementing a successful marketing campaign. How and where do you find these experts, and what do you need to ask before you hire them?

In some cases, your agency might be well equipped. Many large general market agencies have multicultural arms with consultants who specialize in particular markets or audiences. Similarly, many smaller general market agencies that operate in markets with large multicultural populations are intimately familiar with those diverse communities. More and more general market agencies are adding multicultural specialization to their roster of services, and some understand that multicultural is becoming mainstream, resulting in a "total market approach" that assumes the "new general market" is a multicultural one.

The safest bet, however, is to turn to a dedicated multicultural agency. There are a growing number of excellent agencies dedicated to the Hispanic, Black, and Asian markets. A dedicated multicultural agency can advise you about your media plans, local ethnic media and resources, packaging, pricing, and positioning your product or service, and can identify unique, grassroots cultural opportunities for that market. Multicultural agencies are also often better prepared than non-multicultural agencies to help you design culturally sound, non-offensive, non-stereotypical materials. Additionally, the agency will be able to offer competitive insights to ensure you're on the correct strategic path to success.

When choosing an agency, it is also important to make sure it has the operational capabilities you need. For example, do you require the agency report into a centralized office; and/or do you require it to work with others in field offices to execute your campaigns? If so, does it have enough staff to do the work? Does it have an ethnic media specialist? How many creative designers are on staff? What is the turnaround time the agency requires for campaign development, revisions and production? These questions will help you get a sense of whether your company and the agency will be a good fit.

Regardless of whether you go with a general market agency with a multicultural arm or a multicultural agency, don't forget to trust your instincts. If what they suggest to you reeks of essentialism and stereotypes, it probably is. Vet the strategy, campaign, and creative with your contacts in the community, and—this cannot be said too many times- DO THE RESEARCH before launching to make sure you are going in the right direction!

Partner with Grassroots organizations

Don't forget the organizations we discussed in the previous chapter! Community-based organizations (CBO's), community leaders, local churches, and local businesses can be extremely useful when trying to reach out to your local multicultural community.

Step 3
Conducting Marketing Research

Reliable consumer research is the cornerstone of every successful marketing strategy. It is a non-negotiable initial step toward planning and implementation, especially if this is your first attempt at marketing to in-language or multicultural groups in a new market.

Think about what it would be like to maneuver your way around an unfamiliar house in the dark. You may be able to get around but not without stumbling over furniture or walking into walls. You cannot really shake that anxious feeling that comes from not being sure of your next step. Research is the light you need to be able to take confident steps in the right direction.

Research can help inform the development of your hypotheses, and allow you to test them before making large-scale investments. But before conducting research, there are important questions to consider: What is the best research approach and methodology? How do you find quality research partners? How can you avoid common research pitfalls that lead to bad decision-making?

Different goals require the application of different research methodologies, and sometimes multi-method research is needed to gain the most actionable insights. This section provides an overview of various methodologies, as well as some insight as to the appropriate research for different situations.

Research options: Primary and Secondary Research

There are several choices when it comes to the kind of research products and services you can purchase. However, when it comes to multicultural research—and in-language research in particular— the resources are fewer; costs may be higher; and identifying a reliable, reputable supplier is essential. Research is divided into two general categories: Primary and Secondary.

Secondary research refers to collecting, analyzing, and reporting information that is already readily available. A good example of secondary research is Census data. The U.S. Census Bureau collects information on a decennial basis from all people living in the U.S. Additionally, the Census Bureau conducts annual community surveys, collecting information from a sample of people across the country. This data is available on the Census website; and, although you did not conduct this research, you can use the data to inform your business plan or marketing strategy. The Pew Center is also another excellent resource for secondary data. You can access data through syndicated market research reports, which consist of statistics or primary consumer data collected by research firms and then sold to interested clients. For example, author Adriana's firm, Horowitz Associates, produces a series of annual, syndicated reports on multicultural consumers and their consumption of television, broadband, and mobile content, services, and technology (www.horowitzassociates.com/studies).

Primary research, on the other hand, refers to the collection and analysis of data that did not yet exist. You can commission your own primary research through a market research provider who can design and implement a study to address your key issues and questions. The data from custom research projects are proprietary to you. Companies use custom market research for a wide variety of purposes:

➤ To inform product development, pricing and packaging; to inform marketing and branding strategies;
➤ To test creative and marketing collateral;
➤ To gauge PR effectiveness;
➤ To benchmark and track key metrics such as brand perceptions, customer satisfaction, and market share, among other applications.

There are many options for the types of methodologies used to collect primary research, and it is important to understand the appropriate application for each. Ideally, you will contract a professional, experienced, and well-regarded market research firm or consultant who will consult with you on your objectives, then advise you on the research methodology and design that will best suit your needs and goals. And for your multicultural marketing strategies, you want to find a vendor who has proven expertise and experience conducting research among the consumers in your target demographic.

Research Methodologies: Quantitative

When we discuss quantitative research, we are usually talking about survey research—via telephone, online, mail, or in person. Through this kind of research, you can get a statistically representative "measure of the market" for your product or service. This methodology can also assist you with identifying potential trends, obstacles and opportunities and identifying consumer profiles and segmentation. In a nutshell, quantitative research answers questions like…

➤ Market Potential

- How many people would be interested in my widget?

- Market Profiling and Segmentation

  - What are the media and demographic profiles of the people who would buy my widget?

  - What is the likelihood that this particular group of people would buy my widget?

  - How do my potential widget buyers consume media?

- Product Development and Positioning

  - Which of these potential widget designs appeal to the most people?

  - Which price point works best for my widget?

  - Which attributes of my widget are most important to the largest number of people?

- The Competitive Market

  - How many people currently own my widget, and how many people own widgets sold by my competitors?

- How many people think my widget brand is better than other widget brands out there?

- What attributes do people assign to my widget brand, compared to the attributes they assign to competing brands?

Costs for quantitative research will vary depending on the methodology selected, the target population (how hard it will be to find the people you want to survey), the sample size (how many people you want to survey), the length of the questionnaire, and the amount and complexity of analysis and reporting that will be required. When requesting a proposal for custom quantitative research, we always recommend getting multiple bids, but you need to compare the bids "apples to apples." For example, one provider may recommend an online approach, another, a phone survey.

Make sure you understand the rationale and implications of each option before making your decision. Online surveys are often cheaper— but are not always the appropriate methodology when trying to reach specific target populations. On the other hand, with more and more young consumers using wireless phones instead of landlines, phone surveys may not be the most effective means of reaching the 35-and-under population.

A good research company will give you various sampling and price options so you can make a decision that fits both your needs and your budget. A multi-modal approach is always a good option if it fits within your budget.

Most importantly, don't choose your vendor on budget alone. We all know we shouldn't compromise on quality—and this applies especially when it comes to research. In quantitative research, quality control needs to be a top priority.

First, the size and composition of the sample (the pool of respondents) needs to pass statistical muster for your data to be representative and valid.

Second, careful attention needs to be paid to the questionnaire design, the wording of the questions, and the scales used for ratings to ensure there are no biases or incorrect frames of reference built into the survey that could potentially render your data meaningless.

Third, the reporting and analysis of the data itself must be accurate and not misleading.

Adriana's notes:

> *As a researcher, I consider it part of my own competitive strategy to respond to any and all invitations I get to participate in surveys so that I see what our competitors are doing.*

> *I can honestly say at least 95% of the online or phone surveys I complete have some sort of structural design problem that*

compromises the accuracy and reliability of the data. One of the most common issues is not allowing the survey respondent a way 'out' of a question.

For example, recently I received an online survey about hotels. In the survey, they asked me to rate a series of hotels on a number of attributes: cleanliness, price, friendliness of the staff, etc., on a 1-10, poor to excellent scale. Yet, it did not give me the option to say, 'I don't know' or 'I can't rate.' If I have not stayed at that hotel recently or don't remember what the stay was like, it would be impossible for me to answer this question accurately, but I didn't have a choice but to choose a random number from 1-10.

If for every four respondents able to rate the attribute accurately, there was one like me who had to randomly pick a number because they were not given an option to say 'don't know,' that would mean 25% of the data collected are inaccurate.

Research Methodologies: Qualitative

Qualitative research is used primarily for exploratory reasons: to uncover issues, reasons, motivations, feelings, opinions, and attitudes. Essentially, this kind of research is used to get "intimate" with a cross-section of people who have been pre-determined to be within your core audience. It answers why rather than who, what, and how many. Qualitative methodologies include focus groups, dyads, triads, one-on-one interviews, and custom market research online communities, among others.

People often question whether qualitative research is "valid" because it usually is conducted among small groups of people, rather than among large samples of respondents.

The answer is a resounding "yes"— when it is used for the right reasons. You would not conduct focus groups to determine what percent of the population is interested in purchasing your product. You would conduct focus groups to get feedback from consumers about the creative execution of different ads to sell your product, what consumers think about your product, or why consumers might choose a competing brand instead of yours.

This kind of information is what you take to the drawing board to help you craft and hone your offering, and it will lead to insights you would never have been able to find from quantitative methodologies.

The following are some key points to keep in mind when conducting qualitative/focus group research:

➢ Be specific about your objectives and design your research accordingly.

- You must have a clear objective in mind and recruitment criteria must be crafted so participants in the research are able to speak to those objectives. The more homogeneous a group is, the more effective it will be at informing the topic at hand and the more successful the research will be for you as a result. For example, let's say you want to conduct focus groups among Hispanics about a fast food advertisement that will be placed on Spanish language TV. You want to know which of three ads would be most effective in getting people to purchase the item. To reach this objective, you want to make sure all the people recruited for the focus groups have at least two things in common: one, they actually eat fast food (preferably from your restaurant or your direct competitors), and two, they watch Spanish language TV.

- Think about this. On the first criteria—being in the category for the product—you might say it would be interesting to hear from people who don't eat fast food about the barriers to doing so. This may be true, but that is another focus group. The real objective here is to test the effectiveness of the ad among potential customers. On that topic, people who don't eat fast food would have nothing to contribute, because nothing would convince them to eat your product. On the second criteria—watching Spanish language TV—the fact is that among Hispanics, the profile of Spanish language TV viewers and English language TV viewers is very different. You don't really care, in this case, about the opinions of people who don't watch Spanish language TV because they're not going to see any of these ads; and their opinions would probably be very different from the opinions of those who would.

- Homogeneity in recruitment also enables the most productive discussions. Let's say you are marketing a clothing brand, and you want to talk to people who wear your brand about what they like about it and to people who do not wear it about why they do not. You should not attempt to accomplish this in one focus group. You need to talk to each consumer segment separately. The conversation you're going to have with those who wear your brand is going to be very different from the one you'll have with those who do not. Half the time, half the group will have nothing to say. You also don't want one type of consumer to influence what the other would say.

➤ Hire an experienced moderator who you like and think would be likeable to the participants.

- Not just anyone can moderate focus groups. There are specific skills and qualities that separate the good from the bad, the experienced from the inexperienced. Good moderators can make participants feel comfortable and open up about anything. They also know how to work the room and control the participants, keeping opinionated, difficult, loud, and influential participants in check while drawing out information from those who are shy, reserved, and insecure.

- Don't worry too much about whether your moderator has "experience" in your category of product or service. While that is certainly a benefit because it will save both of you the time required to get the moderator familiar with the product category, in reality there's little difference between the skills needed to talk to someone about food products, entertainment services, or health care. Remember, it's not the job of the moderator to inform or educate participants about the topic—it's the moderator's job to get the participants to discuss it openly.

- Don't pick your moderator by reading about his or her experience on a resume. Talk to the moderator; if possible, meet with him or her in person. Don't discount your own gut feeling when selecting who should run your groups. Likeability and relate-ability are both very important. If you are turned off by, feel uncomfortable around, or just generally don't get a positive vibe from the moderator, it's likely the participants will feel the same, regardless of how impressive a moderator's resume might look. Also, pay attention to how well the moderator listens to you—it's an indication of how well the moderator will listen to the participants, which is key to establishing rapport during the focus group.

- ➢ Don't be penny-wise and pound-foolish.

  - • Even though it's qualitative, not quantitative, be careful not to skimp when it comes to the number of groups or participants you include in your research. For focus groups, dyads, and triads, it is important to duplicate your efforts to ensure what you hear in one group was not simply a fluke. Using the example of the clothing brand, you should not convene just one group of people who wear your brand and one of those who do not—you need at least two groups of each, and preferably, visit more than one market to make sure what you hear in one part of the country is the same as what you hear in another. If budget is a concern, let your market research consultants know your budget, and ask them to provide options from which you can choose, indicating the benefits and drawbacks of each scenario.

- Similar to that of quantitative research, the budget for qualitative research depends on a number of factors. Although pricing is usually per group when it comes to focus groups, conducting two groups in one day in one facility will always result in a lower per-group cost than conducting one group per day over two days. For one-on-one interviews, pricing is usually per interview or per diem. Targeting harder-to-find populations, in-language moderating and translating, or more sensitive subject matters usually requires higher budgets. For market research online communities, the price will include recruitment of the participants, the development, licensing and maintenance of the portal, the duration of the community (from a few weeks to ongoing), how often and how much moderation the community will require, and how much reporting will be required. The size of the community (in terms of number of participants) is another key factor. Almost always, participants in qualitative research receive a financial incentive to participate.

➢ Understand the flow and energy of focus groups.

- Focus groups are generally scheduled as 1 ½ hour sessions with 8-10 participants, during which the moderator will guide the participants through a discussion of the topics you want to cover. Prior to the groups, you will work with your moderator to come up with what is usually called a "moderator's guide," an outline of the topics, specific questions, and often, exploratory exercises the moderator will use to draw as many insights as possible from the participants. These discussion guides should not be designed to generate "yes" or "no" answers. Remember the point of this is to engage in discussions, not to quantify responses (for answers to "yes" or "no" questions, you'd be better off doing a quantitative survey).

- The first 10-15 minutes of the focus group is usually devoted to breaking the ice. The moderator will encourage the participants to introduce themselves and will usually lead with some very broad discussion topics to get a sense of where all the participants stand on the issues to be discussed in the group. From there, the flow of the focus group will progress from broad to more narrow and specific. Exercises, games, and visual aids may be used throughout to generate feedback and free flow of ideas.

- Consider the time limitations and the flow of the group when deciding what topics to cover, and resist the urge to try to get answers to every question you may have about your product or brand during one focus group. Remember, because of the qualitative, discussion-oriented nature of focus groups, each participant gets a turn answering or addressing each question or topic; and some participants will be more long-winded than others. A good moderator will have well-honed time-management skills, will be able to advise you on the breadth and depth she or he will be able to cover, and will work with you in determining which topics are the highest priorities and which may need to be sacrificed if time is short.

- Remember each group will be different due to the personalities, backgrounds, and opinions of the participants; the chemistry between them; and the chemistry between the participants and the moderator. Some groups are high energy, loud, boisterous, and entertaining, while others are more cerebral and low-key. Almost always, there are one or two participants who try to hijack the group by taking over the conversation and one or two that are more introverted. A good moderator will know how and when to silence the "loudmouths" without being insulting and draw the quieter participants out of their shells. Not often, but occasionally, no matter how skilled your moderator, you might have a disappointing group, where the participants just don't have that much to contribute and the energy is low (another reason why duplication of the groups is important).

➢ Be an active participant in planning the groups with your research company or moderator.

- The research company/moderator with whom you are working wants nothing but your complete satisfaction. Of course, there is no way your research company can guarantee how the data will come out— whether the findings will be positive or negative for your company. However, the more input you provide in terms of what you want to learn, why, and how you will be using the information, the better prepared your provider will be to hone the research to meet your objectives and deliver a quality research project.

Communication is important, from establishing the recruitment criteria for who will be in the groups, to determining the topics to cover, to ensuring that the end report is designed to fit your needs.

- Do your best to attend each group instead of merely relying on the moderator's report. Then sit back and relax! Listen, learn, and take notes. You'll be surprised at how valuable and powerful the consumer voice can be and how excited people are to be able to share their opinions and thoughts with you!

Research methodologies: Observational

There are a slew of research methodologies that could be categorized as "observational," including mechanical methods like Nielsen's system for measuring what people watch on

TV. For the purposes of this handbook, however, we are focusing on long or short-term ethnography and videography.

Ethnography means observing the research subjects in their own settings and gaining an in-depth understanding of where, when, and how consumers do the things they do. Ethnography provides **context** to actions, behaviors, habits, and attitudes, because it takes place in the subjects' natural habitats— be it their home, the shopping mall, their community, or now, virtually, through a technique called mobile ethnography. This kind of observation provides a "real-life" understanding of the issues surrounding the purchase, adoption, and usage of your product or service.

Traditional (academic) ethnographic research implies a longer-term project in which the researcher can establish a rapport with the research subjects and is able to observe how behaviors and attitudes change over time – a product of both circumstance as well as the deepening level of comfort and openness the subject has with the researcher. If you're thinking, "this sounds like it takes a lot of time and effort," you're right. Ideally, the minimum amount of time a real ethnographic project takes is about 7-9 months, with at least 6 months, if not more, in the field with the participants, visiting with each participant on a frequent basis throughout the study.

Because of the investment of time and money required for "real" ethnography, shorter-term ethnographic projects have become popular. Rather than spending 6 months or more conducting multiple observations of the participants, researchers visit each participant fewer times—in some cases only once—and over a smaller span of time. Short-term observational research is a compromise compared to "true" ethnography; but by visiting with people in their own homes, surrounded by their own families, objects, and possessions, you can glean invaluable insights about how brands, products, and services are integrated into their daily lives and how their behavior is impacted and shaped by their lifestyles and circumstances.

Adriana's notes:

An example of an in-home observational project Horowitz and Associates conducted consisted of a series of in-home visits among Latino families in Los Angeles and New York City.

The goal of the research was to understand how the household managed television viewing when there were some members of the households who were Spanish-language dependent and others who were more English-oriented or bilingual. Even though we only conducted one visit in each of thirty homes, we were able to glean really interesting insights on how language impacts television-viewing choices in bi-lingual households. For example, when watching TV together, families often watched in English because the American born kids preferred it. However, they would select slapstick comedies, action movies, or reality shows over programming with heavy dialogues because these shows would be more easily understood by household members that were not fluent in English.

An example of the use of videography is our "Viewing the Viewer" study, which we present at our annual Multicultural Forums held in New York City each spring. The goals of "Viewing the Viewer" are to understand multicultural consumers' attitudes towards in-language and culturally relevant content, diversity in mainstream media, television-related social media, new entertainment and telecommunications technologies.

The 8 Principles of Multicultural Research

Adriana outlines 8 principles of Multicultural Research, which are as follows:

> Principle #1: Bring the conversation to the table. Be proactive. There is always a multicultural story. Find it.

> Principle #2: Check your assumptions and stereotypes at the door. Avoid useless generalizations that obscure real motivations, perspectives, and experiences.

> Principle #3: Look at the big picture first and then approach your target demographic. Multicultural audiences are complex and diverse. To market successfully to one segment of a community, you must understand the community as a whole and how all the elements fit together.

> Principle #4: Learn what acculturation really means–and what it does not. Acculturation is the process of change when one cultural group comes in contact with another.

Through acculturation, both cultures are changed over time. Acculturation really means the creation of a new layer of identity. Unlike assimilation, acculturation implies retention of the original culture as well as adoption of the new. Various researchers claim to use a variety of complex analytics to "predict" acculturation levels, but the most telling marker is language affinity and usage. Less acculturated segments are more likely to speak and rely on the native language; more acculturated segments are more likely to be bilingual or English-oriented.

➢ Principle #5: Keep in mind the impact of diversity within diversity. Multicultural households are multigenerational and multilingual, with varying and ever-changing levels of acculturation. For example, what may be true for foreign-born parents is not likely to be true for U.S. born kids and teens. Similarly, what may be true for the parent that stays home may not be true for the parent who works outside the home.

- ➤ Principle #6: What's true in one market may not be true in another. The only legitimate reason to do research in just one market is if your product is only targeted to that market. If the research is meant to be reflective of a broader audience, then you need to include multiple markets in the research plan.

- ➤ Principle #7: People don't live in boxes. Think outside of the box. We are not defined only by our race or ethnicity. There are many aspects of our lives that define us and different ways we bond with others beyond our demographic characteristics. Consequently, some products and services are actually more appropriately marketed to psychographic segments, not racial or ethnic ones. Think about how Hip Hop music and Anime games appeal to a much broader audience than just Blacks or

Asians or how Latin flavors are influencing the traditional "American" palate. In essence, multicultural audiences are not the "other." They are members of the general market community as well as their ethnic community.

➤ Principle #8: Multicultural America IS America. Multicultural audiences will make up the majority of America, and already do in many urban markets. If your audience is young, then your audience is multicultural. The new general market is, by definition, multicultural. The results of the 2012 election are clear evidence of this new reality.

You can view the 8 principles in PowerPoint format at http://adrianablogs.blogspot.com/.

Step 4:
Preparing a Marketing Plan

Okay, you have identified your objectives, selected your marketing and advertising partners, and conducted the marketing research. The next step is to design your marketing and advertising plan.

Thinking outside the box is essential because many of the basic rules of thumb used in the general market no longer apply in the multicultural one. For example, many ethnic television programmers and radio stations are not Nielsen or Arbitron-rated. What media is available? What other ways are there to spread information to your target community in this specific market?

A marketing and advertising plan should outline both a specific set of business goals and a clear and specific strategy for how those goals will be achieved. Included in your plan should be a budget, examples of the efforts you will undertake to identify and quantify customers, and your ideas for how you will connect with them in a culturally sound way.

You will likely have to present this marketing plan to your superiors in order to get approval.

Here we break down a few, easy-to-follow steps to create a winning marketing and advertising plan presentation. Each company may require different formats or what is required in the plan, but the following sections will give you a good start. The length of each section is dependent on each company's internal procedures.

➢ Section 1: Executive Overview

- Briefly state the major points of your plan, using bullet point lists and short sentences.

- Include a description of the product or service you will be promoting in the plan and the financial numbers/rationale behind your idea.

- Provide an overview of the target audience(s) for the plan.

- If possible, keep this section limited to a single page.

➢ Section 2: Strengths, Weaknesses, Opportunities, and Threats Assessment (SWOT)

- A SWOT assessment provides a 360-degree, full-color picture of the market for the product or service you are selling and your company's competitive positioning as a provider of that product. This analysis will help you to understand and explain the competitive landscape while providing the rationale for your marketing and advertising plan. Further, a well-developed SWOT assessment will provide guidance for designing the advertising strategy, establishing product pricing and positioning, and selling your product in a competitive environment.

- Include in the SWOT assessment as much background data as you can find, such as financial and sales reports on current products, demographics of your target audience, and information about your competitors' products and pricing.

- When working on a SWOT, the first step is to outline your company and products' STRENGTHS against the competition. Think about product penetration, pricing, packaging, location and customer support. This helps you to recognize where the company stands and what you can focus on, as well as to market your message about how you are better than the competition. This will vary based on the ethnic group you are targeting and what your competition is offering to gain those customers. For example, the consumer segment or segments you are targeting with this plan could potentially fall in the "strengths" category, because they are your core customers.

- It is important you understand where your WEAKNESSES are regarding product superiority, pricing, customer care and availability. This, too, may vary by ethnic group/language segment; and understanding those subtleties is key. For example, a widget that is viewed by a younger, more technologically savvy consumer as superior because it is very high tech may be difficult for an older consumer to use, particularly if that consumer's main language is not English and the widget's instruction manual is in English only. This analysis of your strengths and weaknesses sounds simplistic, but it is a crucial step towards understanding how to improve your product or, at least, how to improve your messaging about your product/service to your target consumers. For example, if the consumer segment you are targeting is a market you have not yet targeted for your product or service, it may be your weakness.

- Consider what future OPPORTUNITIES there are to continue growing and to become the leader within the industry. Is it an influx of new immigrants in the marketplace? Is it technology? Social media continues to grow and develop, allowing for new marketing opportunities daily. As we have discussed, most ethnic groups over-index on usage of the Internet and are early adopters of new technology to enhance their lives. Is this an area your company can gain traction? So, if the product or service would enjoy substantial growth among those consumers you are targeting, that identifies an opportunity. Natalie points out; "We are going through a generational shift - from a generation that values ownership to a generation that values access." This is something your company needs to think about and address based on your product or service.

- Finally, you must understand who or what are the current and future THREATS to your success. Threats could come from current competitors, future competitors, shifting technologies, shifting consumer expectations, or new products coming into the marketplace. Examples of some immediate questions you must address include:

  - How does your pricing compare to your competition? Are you more expensive?

  - If your competition has a larger marketing budget, they probably have a larger "share of voice" (SOV) in the marketplace. If they are outspending you 12:1, then you have an issue with your marketing budget and will have to find creative ways to make your dollar reach further and gain SOV.

- What challenges will you face from sales, distribution, fulfillment, and support perspectives? How do your competitors stack up in those areas?

- If you are targeting an in-language demographic and your competitors provide services for language dependent/preferred customers but you do not, this will be a threat to your potential success.

➤ Section 3: Business Goals and Objectives

- The measurement of success is the attainment of specific, well-defined goals. A key component of your presentation is the definition and justification of your goals and objectives. These goals need to be specific, measurable, results-oriented and time-bound. For example, "In the first year we want to increase penetration to 10% in the Chinese market." Or, "We want to increase sales with this product/service so that revenue reaches $500,000 per year, within 2 years."

- Presumably, these goals should be aligned with your overall business, marketing, and sales objectives. If this is the case, plan to include a detailed description of how this marketing plan will tie in with the company's overall marketing strategy.

➤ Section 4: Target Audience

- This section will define in detail the audience you are targeting with your marketing plan. Use this section to explain and justify the consumer segments you are targeting for your product or service.

- Remember to be specific and accurate. For example, do not say you are targeting "Hispanics" if you are really targeting Spanish-speaking Hispanics with a Spanish language campaign using Spanish language media. That would mean you are specifically NOT targeting U.S. born Hispanics that tend to consume less Spanish language media and more English language media. Similarly, do not say you are targeting "Asians" when your target is the local Japanese community.

➢ Section 5: Product/Pricing Strategy

- In this section, outline how and why your product and pricing strategies make business sense and how you will be positioned in the competitive environment.

- The product strategy should give a detailed description of what your product(s) are and why the ethnic markets you are targeting will buy it. Here you should include any data or research you might have that indicates why and how this ethnic community is going to use your product/service, especially if there are unique cultural or lifestyle factors that make the product particularly relevant to this community.

- Provide a competitive overview about how you stack up against other companies in the same space. While this may overlap somewhat with information in the SWOT assessment section, here you should outline your strategy to directly address those key competitive issues.

- The price strategy is a crucial aspect of the plan. Use this space to explain and justify the price-value strategy. For example, if your product is priced high but you believe it will have high value to this segment that will justify the cost, explain that here. On the other hand, if you are taking the low cost approach, explain how your company will succeed with the low profit margin.

- ➢ Section 6: Advertising and Media Strategy

  - • This section covers your plans for branding, positioning, direct marketing, media, and public relations. An advertising strategy should support the marketing plan, which in turn will support the company business plan and goals. Of course, you will have to accomplish this within a budget. Use this section to outline your media plan, which may include any or all of the following:

    - • Traditional media such as radio, television, and print, including general market as well as in-language, culturally relevant media;

- New media such as online, mobile, and other interactive platforms;

- Social media;

- Out-of-home media such as billboards, ads on public transportation, etc.;

- Event sponsorships;

- Guerilla marketing (recruit real people to get the word out about your company and product, and think about implementing non-traditional tactics, like flashmobs and other creative, unexpected means to get your message out); and

- PR events and releases.

➢ Section 7: Budget

- This section will outline your financial budget. Do your homework accurately and in as detailed a fashion as possible. Break down the budget into specific buckets such as the acquisition cost to gain one new customer, media expenses, events, overhead costs, etc.

- As necessary, provide details as to how the budget may be modified to include additional target audiences or additional media buys, cut back certain "nice to have" elements, etc. so the budget doesn't become the deal-breaker for moving forward and so you can quickly adjust if needed at any point during the implementation of this plan.

- By tracking your marketing costs along with your results, you can calculate your ROI (return on investment)—a core metric in measuring your campaign's success. It is important to track your marketing costs so you can see the results of the number of sales the campaign produced and in-turn this will provide a ROI.

Step 8:
Timeline

A timeline or schedule keeps you, your internal team, and your external vendors on track and makes your expectations about deliverables clear.

Formats vary by company, but some type of project calendar is required for the entirety of the campaign that includes the periods immediately before it commences and after it ends.

Provide timelines for reaching specific goals, for example, research, new customers identified, creative and artwork due dates, traffic media deadlines, and results data due for back end analysis.

Chapter 5:
Implement and Execute: Product, Brand Positioning, & Creative Execution

The next step for your multicultural marketing campaign is to determine the way in which you should position your product and brand to your target market and handle the creative execution of your campaign. Although there is a fine line between the two, there is a major difference between a message that resonates culturally and one that plays on cultural stereotypes. Does the agency you are working with know the difference? Do you know the difference?

Product, Brand Positioning and Creative Execution

Not only is your goal to be culturally relevant but also to be true to your brand and image. Why? Your company has made a huge investment in building a brand. Multicultural consumers, like everyone else, are exposed to "mainstream" media every single day, whether in the newspaper, on TV, billboards, the radio, or supermarket aisles. Don't waste that investment! Instead, build on it by crafting or shifting the messaging to be relevant while still maintaining brand consistency. Moreover, if you attempt to redefine your brand completely for a particular audience, you could be perceived as disingenuous.

At the same time, carefully consider what these consumers know and think about your brand, and what you want or need them to know and think— especially if you are targeting in-language segments of ethnic communities. For many recently arrived immigrants who come to the U.S. with little familiarity about, and no relationship with, many American brands and retailers, word of mouth is one of the main ways they decide which brands to trust and which retailers to patronize. Also, financial and legal factors, such as whether or not they have established credit, carry credit cards, have a social security number or maintain formal banking relationships can influence purchase decisions as well. Therefore, their perception about your pricing, payment plan options, and ID/credit-verifying procedures can also come into play.

Part of the value of an investment in research is to understand how consumers in your target audience relate to your brand. What does the community say about you? What is your reputation? What are the attributes that they ascribe to your brand and your products as a result? What are their barriers to purchasing your products? It is a mistake to assume that what people know and think about your brand in the "general market" is the same as what people in different ethnic communities know and think. Good research will help you and your agency to understand better how to position yourself in relation to this community and how best to develop the creative materials for that particular market. You can also take advantage of the research to test the creative materials prior to rolling them out.

An important question is whether or not the customer would choose your product based on product-centric or brand-centric attributes. How relevant is your brand in the decision making process for the customer? Can the product drive sales in and of itself, or is your brand reputation going to play a role?

For example, a pre-paid phone card can sell itself based on the value of the product: the number of minutes it offers for the price, which countries can be called, and the amount of additional charges tacked on to the cost of the card. In this case, the brand often plays little role in the decision-making process. On the other hand, when selecting a soft drink in the supermarket aisle, brand image and loyalty will likely play a role in whether someone will choose Coca-Cola or Pepsi.

The bottom line is that your brand and product positioning and the supporting creative materials should be culturally sound for the ethnic group you're targeting but must also be true to your company branding. This can be tricky to execute appropriately. Here are some "dos and don'ts":

> **DON'T** attempt to target an ethnic community with an in-language campaign that is essentially your general market materials translated word for word. **DO** look to your agency to help you redesign the materials to ensure the positioning and messaging will actually work for this market and do not contain anything potentially offensive or stereotypical.

➢ **DON'T** completely reinvent your brand to be more palatable for one particular ethnic community. **DO** identify those particular brand attributes that happen to resonate the most with that community, and use those as a foundation for your targeted messaging. Stay true to your brand, with a focus on cultural relevancy to your target audience.

➢ **DON'T** underestimate the sophistication of your target audience, and **DO** pay careful attention to the information you provide around pricing and offer positioning. If you have a compelling, competitive price story to tell, make sure it is articulated in a clear, easy-to-understand, cultural and truthful way. Much too often, campaigns targeting in-language communities include offers that sound too good to be true or that are too complicated and convoluted, with key details hidden in the fine print. Consumers of any race or ethnicity might fall for that once, but these kinds of tactics do not lead to customer loyalty.

➢ **DON'T** be blinded by the competition. **DO** your homework. Make sure you have researched who your competitors are and what they offer to this consumer segment. Leave your ego at the door when comparing your product to understand completely what the benefits and drawbacks are of their product compared to yours. What is your price/value relationship? What is theirs? What about your product would make it more appealing to these consumers? Do you offer better quality? A better value? If you don't know, it's time to do some research on your competitive environment.

➢ **DON'T** forget to inform your sales and support staff about the campaign. **DO** make sure that your staff is aware of any materials that potential customers are seeing and that they understand the specifics and nuances in the messaging. Remember, they are a live extension of the campaign materials; and the message they give to customers must be consistent.

➢ **DON'T** simply slap on a flag or fill in your fonts with flag colors as this could potentially come off as a lazy attempt at being culturally relevant and ultimately backfire.

➢ **DON'T** make the mistake of confusing cultural sensitivity with stereotypes. How many times have you seen marketing materials targeting the Asian community using Japanese-looking fonts, or Hispanic-targeted materials featuring a Mexican "sombrero"? These are simplistic, essentialist, and rather stereotypical. A good agency will know how to introduce cultural cues subtly into your creative so that it comes off as inclusive and relevant, not condescending and offensive.

Below, Natalie describes a successful, very culturally relevant campaign she developed to promote High Speed Internet subscriptions to the Asian market.

Natalie's notes:

I was developing a campaign to increase subscriptions for High Speed Internet and gain penetration into multiple Asian ethnic groups, primarily second generation. Our goals for this campaign were to increase awareness about the product, educate the market about the features and benefits, and find a unique way to reach this audience in a culturally relevant way to get this message across.

We decided to use Boba drink sleeves to advertise this product. What is a Boba sleeve, you ask? Well, a Boba sleeve is similar to the cardboard sleeves you get at Starbucks to protect your hands from a hot cup of coffee. In this instance, it is used around the cups in which Boba drinks are served. Boba teas or drinks originated in Taiwan and today are very popular among virtually all Asian groups. The name for these tea-based drinks comes from the fact that they are usually served with tapioca "pearls" or balls on the bottom. The tea is served either hot or cold, and often flavored with fruit, fruit syrups, and milk. Today Boba shops are popping up in virtually all cities across the U.S., catering to both Asian and non-Asian customers; but this is a fairly recent phenomenon. For years, and certainly when we launched this campaign, you could only find Boba Tea shops in heavily populated Asian communities. We created these wonderful sleeves that were produced in 4-color and included a photograph of a young Asian woman with a laptop computer and culturally sound messaging about our High Speed Internet service.

We then distributed these Boba sleeves to various Boba Tea shops in the area and contracted with them to slip the sleeve on every Boba drink they sold. They were happy to partner with us on this because they didn't have the hard cost of buying the sleeves themselves, and were thrilled that a Fortune 50 Company was taking steps to reach out to the community in a culturally sound way. We knew these Boba sleeves would literally be right in the hands of the exact customers we wanted to reach. The campaign was incredibly successful and provided the company with acknowledgment within the community as a company that cared. The company earned respect and, in turn, reached new customers and new subscriptions; and this loyalty has continued ever since.

Media Buying

Not all media will work as successfully for one cultural group as another. As with all successful marketing plans, it's important to make sure you have the best media mix to reach the target audience and to spend your budget wisely. This can be challenging, especially because, as noted earlier, a good deal of ethnic media is not rated by major agencies like Nielsen or Arbitron. Most of the Hispanic media is rated in the US, but most other in-language media is not rated at all. That being said, just because they are not rated does not mean that they are not important vehicles for reaching your target ethnic community. Your multicultural agency will be able to guide you in this arena. Also, reach out and ask your employees from these communities, as they will usually have great feedback!

Don't give up if your options seem limited. For example, if you don't have a local, in-language media in which to advertise, there may be a national publication, an in-language TV channel with a national feed, Internet Protocol TV networks, a website, or a national radio station on which you can advertise to reach your target audience.

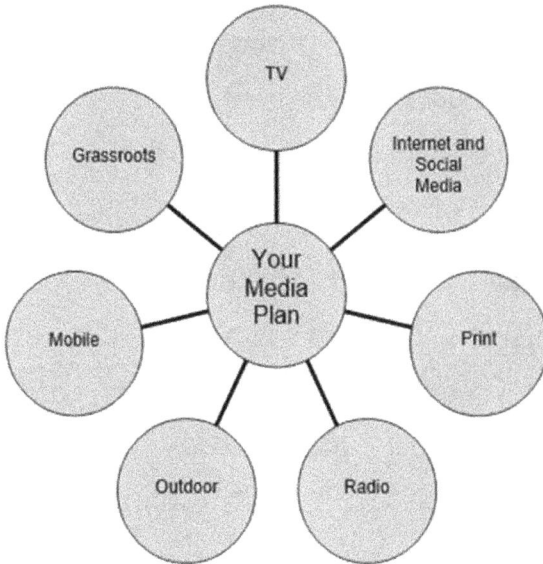

Direct mail can still be an effective tactic, especially if you can reach a linguistically isolated household with an in-language campaign. There are important caveats about direct mail and many new digital ways of getting to your customers, so we recommend you do not rely solely on direct mail to get your message across.

One important caveat about direct mail is that reliable, accurate ethnic data is very difficult to find. Often, households are tagged in your company's internal database as in-language even though no one in that home *actually* speaks the language.

For example, someone along the line may have just assumed that because the household last name is Chinese, it is a Chinese-speaking home! Therefore, you may want to consider bilingual direct mail pieces which will accomplish two tasks: First, even if no one in the home speaks the language, your investment in marketing to them will not be a complete waste. Second, the non-foreign-language speakers in the home will also be able to read the piece. This is important because often the kids and young adults in these households are key influencers or even decision-makers, guiding the purchasing decisions that their less acculturated parents may make.

Don't just rely on traditional media. Work with your agency and your internal team to put together the best mix of traditional media outlets, new media outlets and technologies, and grassroots alternatives. Don't be afraid to get creative and find new ways to communicate with your target audience.

There are some sure bets when it comes to the media mix for certain in-language audiences:

➢ Hispanic/Latino:

- Spanish language radio: When targeting Spanish-speaking Hispanics, radio is still a very powerful medium. In fact, in many markets, Spanish language radio (along with Black/urban radio stations) tops the ratings charts, garnering more total listeners than mainstream, "general market" stations. Moreover, Spanish language radio appeals to Latinos across acculturation groups, so using radio is an effective way to send your message, not only to the Spanish dominant segment of the Hispanic market but also to bilingual and even English language Latinos as well.

- Television: If you can afford this kind of investment, there are two major national broadcasters that serve the Spanish-speaking Hispanic audience-- Univision and Telemundo, both with very strong local affiliates across the country. These networks generate extremely high ratings, driven by their newscasts, "Novellas" (Spanish language soap operas), and sports programming. There are also many other national networks that reach households via cable and satellite distribution that can reach your target audience.

- Cable: Don't discount smaller Spanish language networks distributed via Satellite or Cable TV. There are as many networks out there as there are countries of origin, plus others that offer specific programming genres (i.e., sports, novellas, movies, children's programming, etc.). Each of these networks serves a targeted and loyal following. Advertising on these networks is much less costly than on the major Spanish language broadcasters and may even be more effective in reaching a particular audience than making an investment with the national broadcaster.

- Sports events, particularly soccer, baseball, boxing, and wrestling.

- Movie theatres, especially family-oriented/children's films, action, and horror movies.

- Websites tied to the major television broadcasters, such as Univision.com and Telemundo.com, as well as social media sites (Did you know there is a Spanish Facebook interface?). Also, consider the websites of newspapers and radio stations from your target's country of origin.

- Mobile apps, particularly games, TV, and social media.

- Churches and community organizations.

- Out-of-home and public transportation.

➢ Chinese:

  - Newspapers and Web Portals: When targeting the foreign-born Chinese community, look to Chinese newspapers and Chinese web portals. This is a language-dominant community that is very interested in connecting with news and happenings back home where they have family and friends. Most major markets that have a large Chinese population will have several newspapers available for the community.

- Cultural events. An example is the Lunar New Year or Autumn Moon Festivals. These events are essential to connect with your Chinese customer. You will have the opportunity to introduce a new product or receive feedback about how you can make the product or service more valuable.

➢ South Asian:

- South Asian websites: South Asians tend to be heavy web users. If you want to find South Asians, speak to South

Asians and sell to South Asians, then you need to be a part of the online community. There are many social media groups specifically for this audience. You should advertise in those social media, and/or you need to become part of their blogging environment.

- Websites about cricket: Cricket is the most popular sport in India, Pakistan, Sri Lanka and Bangladesh. The majority of South Asian households watch cricket, so you have a targeted audience that will tune in for days. Yes.... I said days! Many of the cricket series will last 5 days and the series or leagues last 6 to 10 weeks.

- Mobile apps, particularly if offers can be scanned or received via text.

- South Asian weekly/monthly newspapers and entertainment

magazines: In this community, new immigrants and first generation households get news, concert information and matrimonial announcements from South Asian newspapers. Matrimonials are very important in these cultures, as the majority of this community still follows the tradition of arranged marriages.

- Cultural events: An example is an event/festival celebrating India Independence. All areas that have a large South Asian population will have an event locally. Beauty Queen events are also another opportunity to reach this community.

➢ Russian:

- Grassroots locations: The Russian community is often tight-knit. Identify Russian neighborhoods; and develop in-language and culturally sound collateral to leave in places such as doctors' offices, local grocery stores selling Russian products, churches and community centers, and building lobbies.

- Social media sites: There are social media sites just like Facebook designed for the Russian community, and those sites are ideal for reaching a wider Russian base.

- Russian music concerts: These concerts are extremely popular and a way to get your branding in front of a very passionate audience. For example, why not sponsor a Russian artist during an upcoming tour?

➢ Filipino:

- Cultural events: Filipino Independence Day celebrations bring the Filipino community together to celebrate this special time of year with food, concerts and celebrities. Being a sponsor and having an on-site presence at these festivals sends a positive message to the community that your company cares about their culture and traditions.

- Filipino celebrity magazines and concerts: Many Filipino television stars are also music celebrities and are huge draws at any Filipino event. Think about partnering with the TV and music companies to sponsor an autograph signing event or celebrity meet-and-greet.

- Television: Filipino TV channels from the Philippines are available via cable or satellite and are a great way to use your advertising dollars to reach this community. Since Filipinos are avid consumers of Filipino television, this is an effective media tactic to reach this space.

Reporting

Throughout the lifespan of the campaign, it is crucial to keep careful records of the results. Which tactics succeeded and which did not? Which creative approaches resonated the best? Overall, what was the campaign's impact on your business' bottom line?

Documenting a campaign's success will help make the business case for multicultural marketing. That being said, if the numbers don't necessarily go your way, don't give up; documenting what went wrong will provide you with insight into what you can improve or change, so you'll be better prepared for the next go-around.

More detailed information about monitoring and reporting your success can be found in chapter seven.

Chapter 6:
Follow Through—Putting your Customer Care Tools & Systems in Place to Meet Demand

Your marketing worked! Next step: Making the Sale.

The customer responded to your marketing efforts? That means you've done a great job so far! But your work is far from over. Are you prepared to turn these potential customers into real customers? When they call or visit your business, can you answer their questions? Can you attend to their needs? Can you make the sale in the language they prefer?

If you can answer YES to these questions, you're in business. On the other hand, if you are not prepared to handle these potential customers when they respond to your marketing efforts, you have dropped the ball.

The process must begin BEFORE you launch your marketing campaign targeted to the in-language populations in your market.

First, it is crucial to instill in your corporate culture the understanding that diversity is not only a new demographic, it is also key to your business' future success. Ensure potential customers get equally excellent treatment— and potential employees the same career opportunities— regardless of the color of their skin, the language they speak or the clothes they wear. If you don't already have a diversity initiative in place, now is a good time to establish one.

Second, and part and parcel of this diversity initiative, should be an effort to hire staff that not only speaks various languages but also understands the various cultures that make up the population in your market—your potential customers. The best approach is to hire from within the communities in your area—the customers you want to serve.

Third, you must ensure there are processes and standards in place so that when customers with specific language needs call or walk into your place of business, they are routed to the company representatives best suited to help them. Why?

Think about it. You have just worked hard to design a campaign in a language that is not English and that is culturally sensitive. You are sending a message that your company is willing and able to communicate with these customers on their terms. You must be able to follow through on that promise.

The audience you are targeting, by definition, is likely not to have nearly as high a comfort level in English as they do in their native language. They may not be proficient enough in English to understand you. Similarly, these potential customers may speak with a thick accent and in broken English. Your English-only staff may have a difficult time understanding them. How can you successfully transact if you cannot successfully communicate?

In many cases, there are cultural nuances that only someone intimately involved with the community would be able to recognize and that someone who simply speaks the language but is not culturally sensitive would not know. For example, did you know that many South Asians expect to be able to bargain to get the best deal? If you don't bargain with them, it may appear your company is inflexible and not really interested in having them as customers.

This may seem like a no-brainer; but in fact, we have seen many excellent multicultural marketing efforts fail not because of the campaign itself but because of the company's inability to handle the response to it.

The sections that follow will provide you with some ideas and guidelines for successful diversity initiatives, hiring from within the community and establishing the systems and processes to ensure that you can, in fact, translate a successful campaign into real business for your company.

Launching a Diversity Initiative and Providing Ongoing Training

A successful diversity initiative accomplishes tangible goals beyond just making diversity a top priority for a short time. Employees at companies that have committed to long-term diversity initiatives have the information and education they need to be able to provide and better serve the diverse customers that want to do business with you. Moreover, a successful diversity initiative helps to ensure all your employees, no matter the color of their skin, their country of origin, their gender, or their sexual orientation, will be encouraged to strive toward success and thrive professionally at your company—making your investment in those employees will really pay off. Ultimately, a well-designed and executed diversity initiative, over time, will ensure your company is poised to compete and excel in a more diverse, multicultural general market.

At the very least, a good diversity initiative includes for all employees ongoing cultural sensitivity and sales training aimed at addressing issues of a diverse workforce. It also includes ongoing workshops to help employees handle potential scenarios with diverse customers and a zero-tolerance policy for culturally insensitive language, behavior, and attitudes.

Cultural sensitivity training can be an important tool and is a valuable investment. It ensures your employees are adequately prepared to serve diverse communities and cultures. For example, a door-to-door sales person with Chinese culture training knows removing shoes or covering them with disposable shoe covers before entering the home is a sign of respect that could mean the difference between making or losing a sale. A well-trained employee can deliver new customers, generate loyalty, and play a crucial role in spreading positive word-of-mouth about your company. A poorly trained employee may, at the very least, provide bad service to a customer, and could unwittingly offend someone. This can instigate a downward spiral of negative PR in the community— and recuperating from that may prove extremely difficult, especially in the early stages of your multicultural outreach.

In the best-case scenario, a diversity initiative takes a holistic view of a company to identify areas of strengths and weaknesses from all perspectives. In addition to the key areas addressed above, a holistic diversity initiative asks, how diverse is upper management? What impact does the diversity, or lack thereof, of key decision makers have on the business decisions that are made? What efforts are in place to mentor and develop non-white junior employees so they can grow into senior positions? What about your product? Does it really meet the needs and expectations of a diverse customer base, or is the expectation that one-size-fits-all? What can be done to make your product more appealing to diverse customers without alienating your current base? And finally, what kind of "vibe" do customers get when they visit your place of business? Is it welcoming for all visitors, or will certain groups feel alienated because of the décor, signage, or any other features?

Hiring from Within the Community

Ideally, to serve communities that speak a language other than English, you should have staff in place to be able to communicate effectively with these valuable customers or potential customers at all points of customer contact

➢ Your sales team
➢ Your team of installers or technicians, if you sell an installed service or product

- ➢ Your customer service/technical support team
- ➢ Your billing team
- ➢ Your management
- ➢ Any other customer contact point

You might be thinking this is a tall order! After all, in most U.S. markets there is a great deal of diversity! To be able to have all of the in-language communities represented, say, in New York, Chicago, Los Angeles, Boston, or many other U.S. cities, you would basically need to have an international staff!

Exactly!

It's really quite simple. Your staff members will reflect the diversity of the communities you serve if they come from those communities. Reaching out to hire from within the ethnic communities you are targeting will accomplish two important goals: One, you'll be able to hire native speakers of the various languages your customers speak; and two, your staff will be cued into cultural nuances you might otherwise miss but are important to know in order to close a sale and provide the best customer experience.

To find these candidates, think outside the box! Go back to your multicultural marketing basics. Before hiring, don't just take a candidate's word; do your due diligence by really checking a candidate's cultural and linguistic fluency.

➢ Advertise in local newspapers and magazines that target specific communities rather than in the mainstream media;

➢ Use word of mouth. Let local community leaders, educators and organizations, as well as your current employees, know that you have openings;

➢ Use bulletin boards and community notices in places such as churches, the local Y and grocery stores to spread the word;

➢ Offer summer internships for young people within the community. This will allow them to get a foot in your door and potentially interest them in a career with your company in the future.

➢ If possible, offer flexible hours to accommodate for family, school and other commitments; and

➢ In all your advertising, make sure you mention "ability to speak Spanish/Mandarin/French/etc. is a plus," When appropriate and feasible, the information in your ad should be in both English and your target language.

Establishing Internal Processes and Standards

Great job! You've gotten this far. You've done the marketing and advertising. You've launched a diversity initiative to ensure your employees are sensitive to the needs of both ethnic customers and potential customers. You've hired a team of employees from within your ethnic communities so you can serve these customers and close the sale. However, your job is not done yet! Are your internal processes in place to make sure that non-English-speaking customers are routed to the employee that can best serve them?

It would be impossible to address every possible scenario in which your employees/products and potential customers might have an opportunity to interface. Instead, we have compiled some things to consider in different sales scenarios.

In Retail Establishments

- In a retail setting, consider all the potential touch points that could either make an in-language customer feel embraced or alienated. Is your promotional and pricing signage easy to understand, or is it heavily text-based? Is it easy to navigate the store if you aren't proficient in English, or would someone feel lost trying to find something without a map and a dictionary? Are your store policies, receipts, and other materials available in-language if the customer needs it?

- When it comes to your employees, can they speak the language of the customers you are expecting to visit? How will these customers know that? For example, many retail organizations make buttons for their employees indicating the language or languages they speak. Are you considering the language issue when you do your store scheduling to ensure that you have adequate coverage of in-language employees, especially at peak times when you would expect an influx of customers with in-language needs? Where are you placing those employees? On the sales floor to help guide customers to the products they need? In the fitting rooms to help with advice and customer service? At the cash register to address issues that come up in completing the sale?

- Don't forget your stockroom employees! If you have launched a marketing campaign for a product targeted to a specific community, do your employees in the stockroom know to keep tabs on those products and make sure the shelves remain full? Language and cultural barriers may prevent some customers from asking for help if they encounter an empty shelf, so you could potentially be leaving those sales on the table (or literally, in your stockroom).

In a Call Center

- When in-language customers pick up the phone to call you, what will their experience be like? How are customers routed to the call center? Do you queue for in-language customers? Do they have to navigate through prompts in English? If you don't queue for these in-language customers, do you have a 3rd party translator service available for your customer service agents to utilize? Do all your representatives know how to transfer a caller to the in-language queue, if necessary, so that if potential customers call the regular queue but cannot be assisted, they do not have call back and end up in the queue again?

- What in-language sales tools do your representatives have? For example, do they have a "cheat sheet" or glossary of terms they would have to know in-language? While you may hire bilingual call center employees, they may not know every word for every product you sell. And, even if they speak a common language, different groups may have different words for the same items. For example, in many Latin American countries the word for battery (as in AA, AAA, and C batteries) is "pila," while in Puerto Rico, they use "bateria."

- Now that you are expecting a higher volume of ethnic, in-language callers, have you adjusted your business expectations accordingly? Make sure all of your senior leaders know these multicultural calls will take a little longer than those from general market customers. Your "average handle time" will go up. Employees handling these calls should not be held to the same standards of productivity as employees answering the English queues.

- Many employees in a call center are paid by commission. Is their commission based on realistic expectations and aligned with the actual products and services you are marketing to these ethnic communities?

In-Home Service or Sales Calls

- If your business requires you to send repair technicians for in-home visits, can you ensure someone who speaks the language will be assigned to that home? Imagine the impact of a language barrier when a customer is trying to explain what is wrong with their service, appliance, etc., to your technician. Investing in bilingual technicians can help avoid additional costly visits to fix mistakes.

- Beyond the basic issue of communication, sending someone who "speaks their language" will help ease your customer's nervousness about opening their home to a stranger, an issue which is becoming more and more pressing in light of current attitudes towards immigration.

<u>On your company website</u>

- How can your in-language customers find you online? Do you at least have an in-language version of your home page and most relevant secondary pages? Is it easy to find the way to the in-language site from your main website, or would someone have to weed through a complicated English-language menu?

- Importantly, if you are advertising and promoting your company at all on in-language websites and social media, you must have a corresponding in-language web presence. Someone clicking an in-language banner ad or link should not be led to an English-language website.

- Once you have an in-language site, do not treat it as the forgotten stepchild of your main website. Make sure it is kept updated and, if possible, populate it with culturally relevant information, not just a translation of the main site.

Devise Internal Communications about Your Marketing Campaigns

This too may seem obvious, but it is often an overlooked step in the process. You have developed a marketing plan, created culturally sound marketing materials, and have a sound media plan in place. You are about to launch a campaign. Have you told your company employees about it?

Just as you would for a campaign launched for the general market, you'll need to train your employees about your new campaign. How will you let your employees know about it? How will you incent them to support it? Most importantly, how will you provide them the language and cultural tools they'll need to be able to serve the particular community you've targeted?

As the people on the front lines, whether in a retail location, door-to-door, or on the phone, your employees need to be informed about the campaign so they can prepare to receive the volume of business you are hoping to generate from it. Consider launching an internal communications campaign to generate excitement, and hold training sessions to educate employees about what to expect when serving these in-language customers.

Chapter 7:
Report and Monitor: Best Practices for Measuring and Tracking the Success of your Campaign

Of course, the main goal of any marketing campaign is to sell. But, when your goal is to reach out for the first time to an ethnic community, you'll need to calibrate your expectations accordingly. You cannot measure your campaign's success by the same standards you would use for one implemented in the general market among consumers already familiar with your brand and product. Set your sights—and the expectations of senior management—on reasonable, approachable, and meaningful goals. Of course, without having any benchmark multicultural marketing campaigns against which you can measure, the biggest challenge is determining exactly what that first goal will be.

Establishing Benchmark Goals

It's important to gather data from the general market side of the business so you are able to index the multicultural success against the company's goals. The more data you can gather to show success, the higher marketing budget you'll be able to justify. Thus you will be able to add resources to continue the journey to grow the ethnic business. If you can, tap into the analysts already on staff to help you create reports in formats senior executives are used to looking at as they track the growth of the company business overall.

Continue to gather demographic information, percentage of growth, penetration growth, and both monthly and annual revenue coming from ethnic communities to show the opportunity that the company must embrace.

Tracking Your Success

Measuring Traffic

Don't wait until after your campaign hits the streets to think about how you can track your success. Make sure you incorporate ways to track the campaign's impact into each of your tactics before implementing them. For example, if the campaign drives visitors to your website, make sure you set up a unique landing page so you can track page views. If you route sales through a call center, use dedicated phone numbers for your campaign to track the call volume. If your marketing campaign involves social media elements, take advantage of available analytics to track likes, tweets, click through rates, overall reach, etc. Finally, when actually making a sale, if you are offering a discount coupon or special pricing, don't just give out generic coupons. Set up specific promotional codes to track campaign/ad response so you know how many customers responded to that specific campaign.

Keep a weekly record of the campaign's traffic, broken down into as much detail as possible by the various tactics and media buys. Not only will this document the overall impact of your campaign and allow you to understand the campaign's life cycle, but it will also allow you to analyze the comparative success of every element of the campaign so you can constantly improve on your strategic and tactical choices.

Measuring Return on Investment (ROI)

Make sure you have a way to track the number of new customers gained or dollars sold because of your campaign.

As marketers, we all must work within our allocated annual budget, so keeping a careful eye on the ROI of any marketing campaign is an important measure of success— for both the campaign itself and for you as its leader. You will find that the ROI on multicultural marketing campaigns are often much higher than for general market campaigns. Multicultural media costs are much lower; and, if it is a segment you have never targeted before, your opportunity to generate greater numbers of new customers is much higher. Documenting this will go a long way in generating support—hopefully in the form of more money allocated to your multicultural marketing budget in the future. Plus, chances are your ROI results will set you apart from the rest, making you the company's "shining star!"

Calculating ROI:

Total Cost of Campaign
Divided by
Net Gain of Customers
Equals Cost per Sale

Tracking growth

Whether your company measures growth by number of customers, sales volume, or any other metric, make sure you set up a system to track your growth. Of course, you want to track growth year-to-date; but don't stop there. Track your growth by campaign, as well as monthly, quarterly, and year over year, analyzed by each new ethnic audience you target. Not only will this document how your multicultural marketing is impacting your company's bottom line, but it will also allow you to identify and ultimately predict future patterns of growth which, in turn, will help you to manage your marketing budget better in the future.

Make sure to graph your data so you will have a great visual presentation to show others your success.

Calculating Growth:

Net Gain

Divided by

Pre-campaign Customer Count

Equals % of Growth

Tracking other key metrics

Different businesses may have other metrics used to measure success. Make sure you have a system in place to track your success by the metrics that matter to senior management in your company!

Natalie's notes:

In the cable industry, subscriber growth is the key metric; and we measure growth by the number of new customers the company has acquired over a given period of time. But other metrics are important as well. For example, we also look at ARPU (Average Revenue Per Unit). For each household that subscribes to cable, we ask ourselves if there another product or service this household would enjoy that would increase the monthly revenue we generate from that home.

We also keep a careful eye on our penetration in a given market. Penetration means how many multicultural households in the area subscribe to our services. For example, if we know there are 60,000 Hispanic homes in a certain market and we have 7,000 Hispanic households subscribing to our services, we know that our Hispanic penetration in that market is 12%.

Finally, we look at retention and churn. Acquiring a new customer is a substantial investment, not only in marketing dollars but also in in-home visits for installations and equipment and technology with which we provision the home. Once we've made that investment, we don't want to lose them, especially not to a competing provider. We keep a careful eye on churn— how many customers we lose in a given period of time—and strategize aggressively against it.

Using Market Research to Benchmark and Track Success

Most successful companies share one thing in common: a commitment to ongoing research to understand and keep their finger on the pulse of their customer. Of course, just as research to inform new product/service development and positioning is essential, so is ongoing tracking research to measure success and identify potential issues and new opportunities.

Your research provider can design a local, regional, or national tracking program that can be implemented on a quarterly, biannual, or annual basis to provide you with key insights on:

➢ Awareness: How many more people are aware of your company/product/service than before?
➢ Brand perception: On a series of attributes, how would these consumers rate your company compared to your competition, and how/why has that changed over time?

- Purchase intention/Market potential: How likely are these consumers to purchase a product from you in the near future? What are the barriers to purchase?
- Customer satisfaction: Among those who are customers of your product or service, how satisfied are they? How likely are they to recommend your company to others (this measure is called "NPS" or "Net Promoter Score")?
- Attitudes and usage: How have your target customers' behaviors/needs/attitudes towards your product category changed over time? With technology changing at the speed of light, how are they using and interacting with media (your advertising vehicles) differently?
- Unmet needs: What new products/services are they looking to purchase in the near future?

Adriana's notes:

As we move toward an America that is, in its essence, multicultural, conducting ongoing research to understand how different segments of multiethnic consumers are responding to your products, messaging, and positioning will be essential for success. The fact of the matter is that as our demographics shift, so too will your market share if you are not ensuring that you remain relevant to all of America's ethnic and racial groups.

If your company has a research tracking program in place, it's time to look at the research plan from a multicultural angle. Is there proper representation of Hispanics, Blacks, and Asians in your sample? Have you made the right methodological decisions to ensure all language segments of those targets are represented? Are these groups segmented out and analyzed in your reporting?

If your company does not do ongoing research but has relied on past successes to dictate future plans, it's time to rethink this strategy. After all, it's a new world out there, Are you ready for the "new general market'?

Chapter 8:
Last Thoughts from Natalie and Adriana

Now that you have some resources to get started in multicultural marketing, it's time to put those resources to use! Remember that different approaches work better for different groups so don't be afraid to mix and match the above information and create something that works best for you and your team. This handbook is a great way to start thinking about multicultural marketing, but be sure to continue doing research since strategies are always changing along with the needs of different target populations.

Finally, Natalie Rouse and Adriana Waterston are always available to address specific questions or concerns, so feel free to contact them at any time.

Good luck!

Natalie Rouse

President and Founder
Southern Cross
International
Experts in Multicultural
Marketing
Tel: 925-207-0178
Email: natrouse@me.com

Natalie Rouse is a multi-award winning, nationally recognized expert in multicultural marketing and product strategy. She brings over 20 years of multicultural marketing, operations, media and international business experience to your organization's projects. Natalie possesses comprehensive experience and intimate working knowledge of the processes, operations and procedures prevalent in Fortune 100 companies.

Natalie developed a Multicultural Marketing Division with a Fortune 50 company and during her tenure grew the business into over $1 Billion in annual revenue. Along the way, she received over 40 national awards for multicultural marketing excellence in recognition of her strategic successes and shares her expertise speaking at industry conferences and events.

Adriana Waterston

Vice President, Marketing and Business Development Horowitz Associates, Inc. Market and Multicultural Research
Tel: 914-834-5999
Email: adrianaw@horowitzassociates.com

Adriana Waterston is a recognized expert on the U.S. Hispanic and multicultural market; she is often quoted in the trade and consumer press and her articles on the topic have been published in various media industry publications. Adriana is often invited to speak at industry events and conferences such as the Hispanic Television Summit and those hosted by National Cable and Telecommunications Association, National Association of Multiethnicity in Communications, Cable and Telecommunications Association for Marketing, the Advertising Research Foundation, and the Association of Hispanic Advertising Agencies, among others. She is also the lead organizer and co-host of the annual Multicultural Media for Multicultural America Forum, a New York City event that draws a crowd of over 350 media and advertising executives, now in its 13th year.

Adriana has been named one of the industry's "Most Influential Minorities in Cable" by Cablefax Magazine, and has received CTAM TAMI award for her work in multicultural marketing.

A seasoned quantitative and qualitative market researcher, Adriana handles project management for select clients, and oversees all the company's multicultural and Latino research endeavors. She has particular expertise in ethnographic research, focus group moderation and one-on-one interviewing. Adriana brings to Horowitz Associates the extensive experience she gained during her tenure as a retail executive specializing in marketing and merchandising in her home town of San Juan, Puerto Rico.